Your Cat Is Your Guide

How your cat helps you with your
spiritual awakening

Sylvie Sterling

Copyright © 2022 Sylvie Sterling
All rights reserved.
ISBN:979-8-9909296-3-0

*„Ask not what you can do for your cat —
but what your cat wants to do for you!"*

Sylvie Sterling

DEDICATION

This book is dedicated to my beautiful and beloved cat Lisa who passed away in summer of 2021. She will always be in my heart.

Lisa was my inspiration in so many ways. She taught me to be myself and to „do my own thing", no matter what anyone said or thought.

Right before she crossed over, I promised her to finish my first book and dedicate it to her. So this book is in loving memory of Lisa.

ACKNOWLEDGEMENT

To my wonderful cat companions Lennie, Lisa, Jamie, Leon, and Sheila. You are my joy and inspiration and I love you all so much!

CONTENTS

WHAT TO EXPECT

Everything I write about in this book is NOT derived from conventional cat book lore or from scientists conducting biological research on cat behavior. Thus, the content of this book differs vastly from what society and science has been trying to tell you about cats.

Much has been written and speculated about cats. People typically think they know everything about our furry little friends.
But they don't.

As a cat whisperer, I go directly to the source:
the cats themselves.

I am presenting you with a collection of knowledge and experience from thousands of conversations I've had with cats and their higher selves.

It has been given to me directly by the cats I spoke with, as well as channeled through the cat collective and my higher guidance.

Everything I teach comes from the cats themselves!

This content may ruffle some feathers among conventional cat lovers, but that is certainly not you.

You are here because you are a lightworker, or a starseed, or an awakening soul. You are ready to listen to the infinite wisdom of your beloved cat.

In this book, I will show you how you can harness the spiritual power of your cat for your own awakening journey.

Your cat wants you to find your voice and follow your purpose so you can make a real difference in your own life, your cat's life, and in the world!

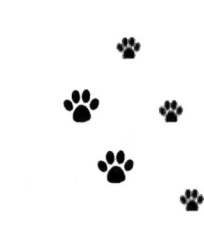

DISCLAIMER

I never use the word „cat owner" because you cannot „own" a cat. Rather, I talk about „their person" or „their human".

Throughout this book, when speaking in singular pronouns, I will refer to cats as „she", although everything pertains to both male and female cats.

For the purpose of keeping it simple, I decided to use the female version. Why? Because cats have something inherently female about them.

This is not about discrediting male cats or getting into a gender discussion. I just want to keep this book simple and easy to read for you.

So if you have a male cat companion, please don't overthink it. Give him a big hug and my regards. He will understand. :-)

Sylvie Sterling

ABOUT THE AUTHOR

H i , I'm Sylvie – your travel guide for this book.

I am a cat expert, cat whisperer, starseed, intuitive healer, spiritual teacher, and awakening coach. My mission is to connect people more deeply with their cats and to guide them on their joint journey of awakening.

Over the years, I've conducted thousands of sessions with cats. All my knowledge, my insights into the cats' psyche and soul, as well as everything I teach comes NOT from outdated book lore, conventional methods, or abstract scientific research.

Everything I talk about comes from the cats themselves!

This book insisted on coming through and was written with the help and guidance of the cat collective, who asked me to pass on their important messages to humans. I am merely the vehicle, the ambassador or the bridge, translating the cats' messages for you. And I am both very excited and very honored to be able to show you the wonderful inner world of your cat, and how she wants to guide you in becoming your best self.

Throughout the book, woven into all the wisdom and teachings of our beloved cats, I also share my own journey of awakening and following my purpose, and how I became a cat whisperer. I hope my story inspires you to also awaken to your full potential, to find your calling, and to recognize how your cat is the secret weapon in your spiritual journey.

I know for a fact that your cat wants you to step up and bring your gifts to the world. Let me and the cats be your guides throughout this book, and get ready for a deep look into your cat's view of the world.

My personal journey: From asleep to awake

Merely ten years ago, I had no idea I would work with cats for a living. I didn't know that I was a starseed, nor that I was a healer, or channeler, or interspecies communicator. I had a regular job as an executive in the entertainment industry, which I really loved, and I went about my normal life. The only thing that I had always known was my inherent and boundless love for cats.

I grew up in a sheltered environment, raised with very conventional standards. For my parents, it was important to be „normal", to not stick out, so that people wouldn't gossip about you. I was taught to follow the rules and just be ordinary – to be a good citizen and a nice girl, and to not look beyond the boundaries of what was considered normal. While I loved and respected my family, I always knew that I did not like to be boxed in or to blend in. On the contrary, from a very early age, I knew I was different.

Somehow I always felt like a fish out of water. I was not interested in the same things other people were. I did not want an ordinary life. I wanted adventure, the unknown, to travel and move abroad. As a matter of fact, I always felt like an outsider in my country, as well as among my friends and family. While I generally got along with most people, I often felt lonely inside. At that age, I didn't know why I didn't fit in, just that I was different.

Little did I know at the time that I was a starseed; now I recognize that I am one of many souls that did nor originate on Earth, but came from a place far far away. We are here to help humanity and mother Earth go through their awakening process and ascend to the next level of consciousness. Today, it all makes sense why I have always felt so out of place. But when I was growing up, none of this information was available. There was no internet or social media, and the libraries had no information on the awakening. Inherently, I took a liking to anything related to stars, science fiction, and space travel. I kept looking up at the sky, wondering what was out there. Now, in hindsight, I know that I was longing to go home, and longing for contact with my cosmic family. But that is a different story for another book.

So in my inner loneliness and feeling different, I turned to the animals. Cats and dogs were the only ones who understood me. I felt most comfortable in their presence and I spent as much time with them as possible. My deep connection to the animals helped me through much of my childhood and teenage years, where I felt disconnected from people. My cats and dogs were my friends, my teachers, and my loyal companions, and they never let me down.

When it was time to choose a profession, instead of following my interest and working with animals, I chose something more „normal" and got into an office job. This eventually turned into a really enjoyable career as a movie executive working for some of the world's biggest entertainment companies. It included international travel, glamorous movie premieres, and many other amenities that came with working in the media industry. It was a fabulous lifestyle, and many people admired what I had built for myself. And I was quite happy with it, for a while... until I wasn't.

While I had spent most of my twenties and thirties nurturing my career, I became more pensive in my forties. What used to tickle my fancy just didn't excite me anymore. Somehow all the glitz and glamour of the media industry became shallow and meaningless. I asked myself what the point of it was, and I wondered if there had to be something more meaningful for me out there. In a life full of amenities and pleasantries, I had built an artificial career-woman persona. However, I was completely disconnected from my true self, my passion, and my purpose.

As a result, my spiritual awakening began in my forties – not with a big bang, but it crept in so slowly that I almost didn't realize it. On the outside, it seemed I was living a „normal" life. But what I was showing to the world was an artificial mask, while on the inside, I felt quite misunderstood – just like I did when I was growing up, and yet, I still refused to settle for the ordinary. I felt a gnawing and a yearning inside of me that I needed to break out, that there was something much bigger and more meaningful to do out there. I just knew that there was something extraordinary waiting for me.

So the adventure of finding my true self began, and it was all thanks to my cats!

PREFACE:
SPIRITUAL AWAKENING

The Great Awakening of humanity is a complex topic, with a lot of different – sometimes contradictory – information circulating within the spiritual community at large. Of course I do not claim to have the one and only truth. As a matter of fact, I believe there is no absolute truth – we all perceive a different reality, and what is true for one person is completely out of the range of what seems possible for the next person.

This book will give you a good understanding of all the ways your cat helps you with your spiritual journey. I will share my definition of „spiritual awakening", so that we are on the same page. In my daily work with clients and their cats, this is what comes up during their spiritual journey.

Your awakening is all about:

Phase 1:

- ✓ Starting to listen inwards and understanding you are so much more than just your body and your mind
- ✓ Realizing that there is an ongoing shift in consciousness on this planet
- ✓ Feeling that we are all connected, and that the universe is a living sea of consciousness

- ✓ Knowing that everything is energy, and that we can influence everything around us with our vibration
- ✓ Understanding that we are all creators of our own reality, with our words, thoughts, and emotions

Phase 2:

- ✓ Tapping into your multi-dimensionality and seeing into other realms beyond the physical
- ✓ Establishing a connecting to the divine and your spirit guides
- ✓ Opening up your higher senses, such as clairvoyance, clairaudience, clairsentience, and telepathy
- ✓ Healing and transmuting your past lifetimes, emotional wounds, karmic burdens, and limiting beliefs
- ✓ Finding and following your calling and life purpose

Phase 3:

- ✓ Fully trusting your intuition, inner knowing, and divine gifts
- ✓ Instinctively following your inner and higher guidance
- ✓ Graciously navigating the shift from our current 3D reality into the 5th dimensional frequencies
- ✓ Settling into your deep connection with your soul family, cosmic roots, and galactic origins
- ✓ Becoming an active part in co-creating the New Earth for all of humanity and every other living being on this planet

As you can see, awakening consists of a multitude of things that will change your life as you know it, or rather, that will turn your life upside down so you can build it back up on a high-vibrational foundation of love, joy, and purpose.

The journey is different for everyone, nuanced by timing and intensity. But the underlying thread of awakening to your fullest potential is very similar for all human beings on this planet.

So far, so good... I am sharing knowledge that you have probably heard from other spiritual channels or many other sources out there. I do not claim to know anything different or spectacular about your ascension process that you cannot find anywhere else.

But what I do claim is that I can help you find your ultimate spiritual guide and your secret weapon for your spiritual journey: your cat!

I will be sharing with you how your cat is going through her own awakening process, and how she wants to actively help you with yours. You will receive many examples of what your cat's behavior means, what she wants you to do, and how she lovingly guides you through the rocky waters of your spiritual journey.

At the end of this book, the cats are sharing their 7-step guidance system for your awakening, and I am adding practical exercises for you to align with your purpose and calling.

Because, ultimately, that is what it's all about: to find your true self and follow your purpose. I want you to know that there is a special gift inside of you, a talent that you are probably aware of but haven't found the courage to embrace. You have a special superpower that is waiting to be shown to the world. This realization is part of your awakening journey.

And the best part is that you don't have to walk this path of discovery and awakening alone – because your cat is right beside you and is volunteering to be your personal guide!

Cat quote:

*„Dear human, everything is well and as it should be in your world. You are making great progress. You are wonderful and can be really proud of yourself. But please enjoy the journey and don't just look forward to arriving. Everything is fine and we are exactly on the right path. You and I, we will do this together. With infinite love for you – **Bibi**."*

Lennie

CHAPTER 1:
CATS & THE AWAKENING

So you are on your own personal path of spiritual awakening and ascension and you are also a cat lover, most likely sharing your home with a beloved feline. But did you know that the two are closely entwined? Cats are not only our furry little friends and loyal companions, they are also helping us with our awakening and our spiritual journey. How exactly they do that will be the main content of this book. But, to set the stage, let us first look deeper into the concept of the New Earth, how I work with it on a daily basis with my clients and their cats, and what future timeline we are moving into.

The New Earth

During this Great Awakening, Mother Earth is raising her vibration and going into higher frequencies. Her heartbeat is being measured daily, in something called the „Schumann resonance". This frequency has been steadily going up for the past 10 years, while the magnetic field has been slowly declining.

As Earth is raising her vibration, so are we. Humans and animals are intrinsically connected to Mother Earth, and when she levels up, we need to catch up!

As a species, we are moving to the next level of consciousness. Some call it the shift from our 3rd dimensional state of being (3D) into the new 5th dimensional (5D) paradigm. Some call it Ascension, some call it the Great Awakening, and some call it the New Earth. Whatever name or label we attribute to it, it's really all the same. The new field of the 5th dimension is already here on Earth, and it is getting stronger every day. When you go into a meditation and imagine hovering above Earth, you can see how the fields of 3D and 5D are both coexisting with and overlaying upon each other, spanning the globe. Truthfully, it is up to us whether we want to keep dwelling in the old matrix of 3D, or uplevel our consciousness to anchor ourselves permanently in the 5th dimensional field. And as more and more people are upleveling and shifting towards 5D, we are co-creating the New Earth together.

Most likely, you have been experiencing the 5D field in various ways. You have access to it when you meditate, do breathwork, do yoga or engage in any other spiritually minded form of exercise. You are definitely in it when you do healing or energy work of any kind. And you are even tapping into it when you do what you love most... when you are in that „zone" where everything is in flow and you are not in your head but in your heart. For some people, that might be when they make music or when they write or paint or create something. For others, it is when they perform their favorite sports or when they are out in nature enjoying the stillness and all the gifts that mother nature has to offer. You are also definitely tapping into the 5D field when you are around animals, when your heart is open and you experience a deep feeling of love and connection with them.

When are we getting to the part about cats specifically? Bear with me, it is coming up very soon.

The bigger picture

Let's keep talking about humans for a little while longer. Each one of us is here to help Earth and humanity ascend to this next level of consciousness and to co-create the New Earth. And while all of us work for the bigger picture – namely, bringing this planet and humanity to fruition and into the higher 5D frequencies – we also all get to put our own personal touch on it. It's just like working for a big company, where everyone collectively works for the thriving and advancement of the company, but the way each employee contributes to this higher goal is vastly different. You need people on all levels and with different skill sets working together, so that the whole company can reach their goals.

It really is the same with humans and the ascension process on Earth. While we all contribute to the whole, our individual souls come with very specific tasks. It is not a coincidence that each one of us is here at this special point in time, and it is by design that most humans have a longing and urge to find their purpose. That being said, every one of us has a slightly different life purpose or soul mission. We are all on our unique path, and have our very unique energetic fingerprint in this world. Visualize it as a big tapestry of life in which we are all interwoven and connected. Each one of us is a patch of this unseen, underlying fabric of life, and we are all woven into this whole and magnificent quilt that makes up the Universe and our reality.

As we are truly all connected and influence each other, each one of us holds one very unique and specific piece of the puzzle. In this way, we can all contribute to the whole of what makes up this Universe we live in.

Your piece of the puzzle

My question to you is: Do you know what your special piece is? Because now is the time to find it and contribute it to the whole! It is definitely time for you to step up and find your calling, your purpose, your superpower, or your special gift.

Most likely, as a reader of this book, you are already on your journey to doing just that. It is not something that happens overnight, and while some people are well aware of their purpose, others might be completely unaware of it or, if they do know it, they may still be struggling with actually living it to the fullest.

Wherever you stand on this journey, know that there is no right or wrong and that you are exactly where you need to be at this moment. There is a reason why our life path sometimes has detours which we will understand much later. There is a saying that I fully agree with: „Life can only be understood backwards; but it must be lived forwards".

With this in mind, don't be discouraged or frustrated if you have not yet found your special calling or if your path is not clear to you. You are already ahead of the curve, because *you are seeking*. This book will shed light on what your calling is and help you understand how to move forward with it. Most importantly, it will help you realize how to harness the power of your cat on your spiritual journey.

At this point in time, much of humanity is still asleep and thinks that their body, their mind, and their earthly existence is all there is. They live in a world of fear and dependency and they believe what they are told by their government, mainstream media, society, and conventional science. As a reader of this book, you have most likely graduated from that state. You are an awakened soul who knows there is a whole different world behind the veil and that we can consciously move into a higher form of living. You may or may not be aware of your piece of the puzzle, but rest assured, there is a breadcrumb trail that shows you the way and we will explore it in this book. Better yet, we will ask your cat for guidance in your quest for finding your purpose and calling. Because now is the time to find your piece!

The New Earth is not a work of fiction. It is already created in the higher dimensional field, and it is right there waiting for us. It is not a new place we are going to, but a higher state of being. Going into 5D does not mean that we are leaving the planet or going through a wormhole. What it means is that we are connecting to that higher-dimensional bandwidth which will enable us to live in peace, prosperity, love, and joy. It is already available for those who know how to access it.

The current ascension process is all about finding our way into the 5D field more often, to recalibrate our auric fields and uplevel our consciousness, so we can stay in the 5D field on a permanent basis. To do that, it is important to keep our frequency up, to connect with the 5D field on a daily basis and stay in it as long as possible. How do we do this? Well, let's look at our little feline companions for help and guidance.

Cats are elevating

Our cats are in our lives for a reason. They are not only with us for companionship. They also want to support and inspire us, and show us the way. Our feline companions are not just little cute animals. They are actually highly evolved divine beings who are by our side for a reason and entrusted with a specific task. The remainder of this book is all about how they help us on our spiritual path, so we can ascend into a higher version of ourselves.

Now that we have touched on the ascension process, let us dive a little deeper. Our world is made up of several layers of consciousness, and also several realms of creation and matter: the mineral kingdom, the crystal kingdom, the plant kingdom, the animal kingdom, the elements, and the human species. While most of these are vibrating on different frequency bands, they are leveling up together with Earth as an entity and a planet. Therefore, it is only natural that the most highly and consciously evolved species – i.e. animals and humans – are elevating as well.

When you see the process in its entirety, it means that not only you as a human being are going through the awakening, but your cat companion is as well! As a matter of fact, our cats are going through the same process that we are: they are expanding their consciousness, becoming more sensitive and empathic, and developing more emotional intelligence and awareness of how everything is connected. Our cats are even suffering from the same ascension symptoms we have: mood swings, oversensitivity, physical issues, emotional stuff bubbling to the surface, and more.

Where they differ from us is that while we humans tend to try and analyze this process and go about it from a thinking angle, our cats are much more tuned into the natural flow of the Universe. As a result, they just allow the process to happen. Cats are very much connected to nature, to their inner guidance, and to divine wisdom. And because they are so much more in tune with their intuition, most of our feline friends are actually ahead of us when it comes to the awakening. While we are blocking ourselves mentally, our cats just go with the flow and allow the experience to happen. This makes them perfect guides and teachers in our own journey.

The role of our cats with us is ever more important!

There is actually a huge difference in cats today from, say, 20 years ago. Just like we humans have evolved in our consciousness and vibration in those 20 years, our cats have as well. We started this process of becoming more compassionate, more emotionally intelligent, and more consciously aware of who we are as human beings, about two decades ago. But it was a slow progression from being asleep and functioning on autopilot, to being an awakening soul who knows there is so much more about us than we grasp with our conventional senses.

By the same token, our cats have also progressed from being cuddly couch companions, or astute hunters following their instincts and living a largely independent life, to being more emotionally intelligent and more consciously awake. Cats are becoming ever more aware of their task with their humans, and how they are here to make their contribution to the betterment of this planet.

Luckily, there is a growing understanding among cat people, and especially in the spiritual communities, that felines are so much more than we were once told they are. More and more people recognize the greatness of their cats, and how their companions came to them for a specific reason. They are beginning to see how their cat spiraled or triggered something in them that was important for their personal development and growth. I feel blessed that I get to work with cats on a daily basis, and I feel honored that I am on the forefront of those telling the world that our cats are actually higher dimensional beings with a beautiful soul and an important task.

Cat quote:

*"I wish for me and my fellow cat that we get to be a part of our humans' awakening. That we are being honored and appreciated for it. That I am not only seen as the `funny little guy', but recognized as a higher being. I am so much more than the sweet and fluffy feline people see in me. I can show them a whole different side of me. This is my wish to my humans. Sending you so much love – **Milo**."*

My personal journey:
From seeking to self-actualization

My own awakening began in 2012, when I first read the book „The Secret". This kickstarted my spiritual journey by helping me understand
that we are not the product of our genes or upbringing, that our past
doesn't have to define us, but instead that we create our own reality,
day by day. This knowing stirred something deep in me and started
me onto a personal quest of self- actualization.

The spiritual communities had expected the big awakening coming with the infamous date of 12-21-2012. They thought it would
come with a landslide and instantly change our lives. Many spiritually minded people were disappointed that December 2012 came and
went without opening up the portals of enlightenment for humanity.
But actually, a shift DID happen, it was just much more subtle than
new agers had expected, and it was the very beginning of the ascension process that we are part of today.

Personally, as of 2012, I found myself very much invested in trying to
„better" myself, in finding ways to improve my old operating system
and „fixing" things that were not working in my life. Since the awakening was still in the early stages, I didn't realize that there is nothing
to be fixed, and that there is nothing wrong with us as we are.

The book shelves in stores were full of self-improvement books, and a
common perception was that we needed to overcome our old patterns
by saying mantras or affirmations and by overwriting our old beliefs
with new ones. I was all in on this quest of self-help, but it turned out
to be quite tedious. It felt like a lot of work and I became tired while
still being set in my old ways and daily routines. For most of my days,
I was still caught in action-reaction patterns, meaning that I reacted
to things that happened in my life (while constantly wanting to have

something different showing up), rather than *creating* the very change that I was longing for by just *being* the change.

So I spent most of my early years of awakening in a trial-and-error mode, finding out what did and did not work for me. What I didn't realize during all that time was that my cats were working their magic behind the scenes for me! With their distinct personalities and the issues they came with, they were secretly training me to step into my purpose to become a cat whisperer – only at the time I was not aware of it. Remember the film „Karate Kid" where Mr. Miyagi trained his student to learn karate by giving him household chores? That is exactly what my cats did with me, symbolically speaking.

At the time, I was no different from all the other concerned cat parents out there: I loved my cats dearly, and all I wanted was for them to be happy. So whenever I saw a sign of my cats not being balanced or happy, I tried to do something about it. For instance, Lisa had constant stomach issues. Lennie kept us up at night with loud meowing. Jamie had an uncontrolled temper, and often got into fights with Lisa. I tried everything so my cats would be happy and healthy – from buying Bach flowers to pheromone therapy, from trying behavioral therapy to clicker training, to hiring a cat psychologist and an animal communicator. Some of it worked, some of it didn't. But my cats pushed me incessantly, and I so dearly wanted to understand why they were not happy. I found myself constantly searching for solutions.

What I didn't understand was the underlying picture: that my life purpose was to work with cats, while I was pretty much wasting my thirties working in my glitzy and glamorous executive job. In order to slowly help me step up to the best version of myself, the Universe had sent me three cats with psychological, emotional, and physical issues so I could train „on the job" to work with cats. It took me a long time to make that connection. Many years later, it clicked for me that especially my youngest – Jamie – had come into my life to help me become a cat whisperer. It was with him that I performed my first energy healing, without even knowing it. It was he who pushed me to find solutions „outside the box". After conventional medicine, home-opathy, and plant medicine weren't working for him, I realized that his physical symptom had an underlying emotion. Once I helped him release the trapped emotion, his year-long colon problems stopped, and he became a healthy cat. After behavioral therapy wasn't work-ing to help with his temper and restlessness, I started to realize that Jamie's behavior might have to do with ME being restless... and after I looked into my own behavior, he became a happier cat!

The clues kept coming together, but it wasn't until 2016 that I followed the path of breadcrumbs to understand what I needed to do: start looking for my life purpose! I finally understood that my cats had come to me for a very important reason, and that they were more closely interwoven with my soul path than I had previously thought. Even more, I realized that my cats were more or less reflections of myself.

Lisa

CHAPTER 2:
YOUR CAT IS YOUR WISDOM TEACHER

I t is still a little known fact that cats are not only fluffy and cuddly little animals that enjoy being with us, eating, sleeping, and playing. The underlying fact is that cats actually come to us with an important purpose. Just like you came to Earth with a mission, so did your cat. In fact, her purpose has a lot to do with helping you find yours and revealing your stumbling blocks along the way.

Cats come to us to help us with our purpose and life path

So it really is no accident that you have exactly this cat in your life at this point in time! Your cat's soul chose to be with you... because she has agreed to help you with whatever you came here to do. Cats come to us to help us with our purpose! And they do this with passion, love and full dedication.

While it is true that cats are largely independent-minded and like to do their own thing... they still know they are in our lives to make a difference and to matter! The common misconception about cats not serving a purpose is actually a cause of grief and frustration among felines.

Dogs, for instance, are known to have a purpose with their owners. People usually get a dog with a specific task in mind like guarding the house, providing protection, or keeping them company. Horses are bought with a specific purpose in mind as well. People want to ride them, or spend time out in nature, or participate in horse-based sports or competitions. So there is most always a purpose or reason for people to get dogs or horses. They call dogs our „best friends", but really they also want to have their share of what dogs or horses have to offer them.

Cats, on the other hand, are brought into our lives for different reasons. Cat people are different from dog people. They think differently. Usually they don't get a cat with a specific „task" in mind that their feline companion is supposed to fulfill. Cat lovers appreciate that cats are full of wonder, and while most people are not actually aware of how much our cats do for us, there is a growing understanding among spiritual people that cats are actually much „bigger" than we are led on to believe.

Cats come to us with very specific tasks

So at this point in the book, I will confirm what you already know: There actually is a purpose for cats in our lives. Cats always come to us with a specific task they help us with. And almost all cats I spoke with were very aware of what they do for their person. They know which role they fulfill for us, and what they are supposed to help us with. A cat's purpose my not be as obvious as a dog's purpose, but I think that is what makes it so special and wonderful.

From the cats' perspective, their biggest frustration is that many humans are not aware of what they are doing for us! So the cats are extremely happy when we reach out to them – be it by means of animal communication or just by intuitively tapping in. And they are more than happy to share with us what it is they help us with.

Here are a few examples of cats' purposes with their humans:

Giving love: This is an obvious one. Some cats are specifically tuned into loving us or teaching us love – for ourselves or others. They like to cuddle and fill our hearts with pure, unconditional love.

Spreading joy: Some cats are naturally funny and like to entertain us – either by playing or making funny antics. They will always help us lighten our mood or make us smile when we feel down.

Healing and energy work: Most cats are natural healers, but there are designated cats that vibrate on a very high healing frequency. Other cats clear and transmute dense energies around us into lighter energies.

Emotional support: Some cats literally help us carry our emotional burdens, and give us support in our daily life. They are always around us and take on our stress in order to alleviate our burdens.

Mirroring us: Many cats come to us as a reflection of ourselves. They will have the same emotional life themes we are struggling with and can thereby help us overcome them.

And so on. This listing of some of our cats' purposes is just a generic blueprint and only the tip of the iceberg. There are many more designated tasks that cats have with their humans – both generic and very specific.

The common thread is: your cat is with you because she wants to help you on your life path, so you can grow and become all that you can be. It might be frustrating for her if you are not aware of how she supports you.

If you truly want to have a happy cat, then it is essential for you to find out what her task is with you so that you can both come together and function as the dream team that you are supposed to be.

Your cat's bigger mission with you

This knowing is not only important in your daily life, but takes on a whole other dimension when it comes to the Great Awakening. On a larger scale, your cat's task is to push you beyond your limits so that you can fully awaken to your true self. So you can become the highest expression of yourself through which you came to Earth to do.

What does that mean? As I already said, our cats are spiritual beings. They are very much connected to their true nature, to their higher selves and the divine. They come with a deep intuitive wisdom, and they are here to help us on our soul path. Many cats are empaths and channelers. They will channel your divine guidance and they instinctively know what your higher path or purpose is.

In particular, they will push you and remind you that it is time for you to level up!

Remember, you come with a designated purpose and calling. And if you are not on track with it, or if you are not aligned with your bigger path, then your cat will let you know! As it is with cats, they can be quite persistent in doing so.

So what is your cat's grander mission at this specific point in time?

- **To awaken you to your purpose – to find it & to follow it.**
- **To get or keep you on track – when you are not aligned with your soul plan.**

Our soul is very much aligned with our life purpose and divine plan. But our human is not always or not fully aware of what that is. And when we are not aware, then we are typically stumbling in our tracks, things don't seem to go right for us, and we find road blocks everywhere. And most of all, we do not feel fulfilled.

From our human perspective, we don't always notice that. In our daily life, we are usually running around, always doing stuff, and dwelling in our heads. We are constantly thinking of what or what not to do, and where we should go next. Many people live in their head, not in their heart. But we don't always notice that we are not aligned and not fulfilled. Life gives us enough sweet spots that we think we are happy... at least superficially. But our soul and our inner being yearns for more – for true fulfillment and living a life full of purpose and meaning.

The good news is that your cat will definitely notice when you are not aligned with your calling and when you are not truly happy – much more so than you ever will. Her soul knows that it is her big mission to get or keep you on purpose. And she will step in and let you know that you are off – whether you like it or not.

Your cat knows you best

She really does! Your cat does not see the outward „you" that you usually present to the world – all groomed and tidy and well-behaved. She knows you inside out, with all your moods, be it high or low. But most of all, your cat looks right past these earthly things, and instead sees YOU – your soul, your core, your essence, the magnificent grand you that you are holding back from the world, because you think you are not worthy or not good enough to show the real YOU.

Most of us humans are so wrapped up in who we made ourselves out to be. A successful business woman, a busy executive, a great mom, a talented teacher, an ambitious salesperson, an astute marketer – whatever label we have attached to ourselves in order to define ourselves in this world. Some of it is real, but most of it is a facade we built up over time. We turned ourselves into „somebody", with a snappy title or a predefined category, so we can fit certain molds and find social acceptance. But that is not who we truly are. We can fool a lot of people with this persona that we have built for ourselves.

But not your cat! She sees you for who you truly are. She doesn't care about the labels you have put on yourself such as coach, lawyer, clerk. Everything that seems flashy and acceptable to society does not mean anything to your cat. Your beloved feline companion looks right past all that outwards stuff and instead perceives right into your soul.

Your cat does not just listen to your words or look into your face, like people do. That is why you cannot fool your cat, or play pretend with her. In truth, your cat feels your emotions and vibration, rather than solely listening to what you say.

Your feline companion will feel your inner upheaval, your emotional blocks, stress, insecurities, and fears. She feels, sees, and senses what you have buried deep down in your subconscious: your childhood programming, your emotional traumas, your fears of rejection and of not being good enough. She sees through the coveting of your shadow side and all the not-so-pleasant aspects of you that are not wanted in society. We have buried these so deeply within ourselves that we are not even aware anymore that they are waiting for us to address them so they can finally heal and leave our body and our field.

The thing with us humans is we are so busy most of the time that we don't even notice we are not happy. We are so buried in our daily hustle and bustle, taking care of this and that. We need to have a job and make money. We need to pay bills and look after our loved ones. We have to put food on the table, pay taxes, help the community, go about our hobbies, think about our parents and children and friends, and and and... it is exhausting just thinking about it! And we are so busy with all of the things we „have to do", that we hardly find any time to just be happy and enjoy ourselves.

Luckily, our cats will step on our toes when they sense we are spiraling down the wrong path. They let us know when we are stressed out and not giving ourselves any room to breathe. Different from humans, cats are very much connected to their feelings, their innermost selves, and their true nature. They can see it clearly when there is something „wrong" in our lives. When we are not in joy and flow or not aligned with what truly makes our heart sing. And our cats will point it out in any way they can!

Your cat will let you know

How does she do that? Well, your cat can be quite relentless when she feels you are not on track. For instance, have you ever noticed that your cat seems to be restless or meowing more than usual? Or perhaps she is overly seeking your attention, maybe hitting you with her paw or wanting to distract you from your work? This kind of behavior usually gets misinterpreted as the cat wanting more attention, when actually it is just the opposite. When your cat seems restless or seeking to get your attention, in 99% of cases, your cat wants to show you that YOU are not in balance.

Any so-called „behavioral problems" are not what they seem. I really don't like that term because the cat does not have a problem. Instead, any kind of strange or alarming behavior is just the cat's attempt to point out that there is something wrong in her life. And in most cases it is not about what's wrong in the cat's life – but what is not going right in YOUR life!

A cat's „behavioral problem" usually has to do with YOU!

Have you noticed any alarming behavior in your cat lately? Maybe emotional outbursts, mood swings, or physical symptoms? Any kind of increased meowing, restlessness, retreating, or stepped up behavior? The likelihood is yes, because the cats are catching the same cosmic energies we are.

They are going through their ascension symptoms just like we are. For us humans, common symptoms of the ascension process are sudden mood swings, increased worrying, feeling unbalanced or noticing odd aches and pains showing up in our body. We are currently subject to heavy cosmic energies and intense solar flares, hitting Earth during this time of change and awakening. So it is not surprising that cats are feeling these energies as well, and going through very similar ascension symptoms.

But during all that, cats are still very much aware of their responsibilities as our ascension guides. They are so much tuned into us that they notice it when we are not aligned or not in balance. And they make it a point in showing us when we are not in line with our soul and life path. How? We will get into this in the next chapter.

Cat quote:

„You are so huge, but you still don't fully see it. You have gone through a great transformation in the last year, and I am very proud of you and the path you chose. Your light inspires others. You are full of love and always look out for others. I wish for you to put yourself first more often. Be huge. Be yourself. Be the bright star that you are. I love you so, so much – ***Snowball.****"*

My personal journey: Receiving my mission

In 2016, the next wave of the awakening hit Earth and humanity, and once again I was right on target with my own spiritual journey. It was much more intense than the last wave, and it really got me going this time! At the time I was still working in my 9-5 job (or rather 9-9 job) as a busy executive in the movie industry. And while I really loved my work, there was a growing and nagging feeling deep inside of me that I wanted to do something more meaningful. It was the typical and profound process of questioning our own existence that everyone goes through at some point in their life. Why am I here? What is the point of all of this? What do I really want to do? What is my life purpose? And why do I feel such an urge to do IT – whatever it is?

Therefore my forties were all about going on a quest of finding my life purpose and aligning myself onto that new path. Luckily, it didn't take me long to find my calling. Once I started thinking and journaling about it, it was almost hitting me upside the head: „What has taken you so long? It has to do with CATS, of course!"

But I was still going about it from the mind and not from my heart. At first, I identified my purpose as „making this a better world for cats", and I was all happy to set out on this task. Over the next years, the wording and meaning behind this statement has changed. But the overall purpose on working with cats has remained with me.

While at first I went about it from my head, I tried to do everything by the book: I studied classic cat psychology and behavioral counseling, and I was busy getting certificates, so I could start this new career with a profound background. I took on the first clients and put myself out there as a cat psychologist. I loved working with cats, and added more and more skills to my repertoire. I learned energy healing, and started to apply it to the cats I worked with. It all seemed to fall in place, and I felt I was helping cats and people live a happier life together. But there still seemed to be something missing. There was a much higher level of cat connection that I was supposed to explore, and it hit me pretty unexpectedly.

The major key to finding my true purpose was my new practice of meditation and connecting to my higher guidance. I loved to ask my higher self and spirit guides for messages or help on my path.

So the big epiphany of what I was meant to do came while I was traveling and visiting my sister-in-law. One day I sat on her bed in a meditative state. Her cat Mystique sat next to me and gave me intense looks, and it hit me that she wanted to talk to me. So I listened in, and I channelled the most amazing message to date that I had received from „above". My cosmic soul family introduced themselves. They connected with me through Mystique, the cat, and told me quite a few things that left me stunned. But at the same time it resonated deeply with what I had always known.

They told me that I was a starseed with feline origins. That I was being watched over and protected by them, and that I had an important task to do: to tell people the higher truth about cats, and how they are entwined with humans. Then they gave me the following message – or let's say handed me my assignment:

„Tell people to not treat cats as babies or kids, but as grown-ups and divine beings.

Most people don't really understand cats, or they go by what they have heard for ages.

Tell them that cats are divine beings that come to them in order to help them become their best selves.

Tell people about their purpose, and that cats help humans find their purpose and help them follow it.

Tell them that humans are very closely related to cats in their DNA, which explains why humans have such a deep bond with cats.

Tell people to treat cats with respect, because it matters. This is how they treat themselves and others."

This channeling experience left me deeply in awe, full of joy and with a wild desire of putting this all into practice. I knew I had a special message for cat lovers and cat parents, and I set out to properly learn animal communication, so I could work even deeper with cats than I had anticipated.

The beautiful thing was that all the cats I spoke to confirmed what I had received in my channeling, so I knew I was definitely on the right track. It was very clear that passing on the felines' message to humanity became my very own beautiful life purpose – my unique fingerprint and my piece of the puzzle in the awakening.

Once I went deep with all of this and connected with cats on a regular basis, the cats opened up to me. I learned that every cat knows exactly what her task with their human is, although in many cases their human is not aware of it. This knowledge opened up the floodgates of what was to come – I would become a spiritual cat whisperer, something I never would have set out to do, but it evolved naturally and became my new state of being.

I would love to say that it was all rainbows and butterflies from that moment on, but I wouldn't serve you right if I brushed over all the obstacles I seemed to hit. To begin, I suffered pain and loss of my old identity. Walking a new path on pure faith came with its own pitfalls.

Because, you see, there was this little thing called „inner work" that needed to be done, which felt like a rocky path to walk in the years to follow. All my limiting beliefs, my childhood programming, and the artificial persona I had built around myself needed to come crumbling down before I could fully embrace the New Me.

So in case you are wondering why your awakening feels so difficult and why you are going through rough times, then let this be your comfort and consolation: *when you awaken to your true self, you have to let go of good in order to get great.* And just like in every good movie, the happy ending does not come in the first five minutes, but two hours later, after the unlikely hero had to go through some suspenseful and dramatic events with a twisted storyline and overcome many obstacles on the glorious path to her happy ending. So you can take comfort in the knowing that your awakening journey is just like the classic hero's journey in every good movie. There needs to be a process of old routines breaking down, new insights shaking up your world, and new companions to be made until you can reach your highest potential and become a more enlightened and happier version of yourself.

That being said, let us see in the next chapter, how your cat shows you where your stumbling blocks are and helps you navigate the bumpy waters of awakening and transmutation.

Jamie

CHAPTER 3:

YOUR CAT IS YOUR MIRROR

Now that we have established how your cat wants to help you on your path and in your awakening, let's talk about how she actually goes about it. Or better yet, how she will inspire and guide you.

This sounds like a sweet thing to do but in the moment it can feel quite the opposite. Your cat will „push" you, sometimes really hard! It is like a wake- up call from your feline so that you get shaken out of your comfort zone.

Your cat's approach to pushing you

There are three main areas of how your cat will push and nudge you to wake up and realize something is „off" in your life. Your cat wants you to look inwards, think about what you REALLY want, and then let go of your old programming, patterns, behaviors, fears, and emotional burdens, in order to reach your highest potential. She wants to help you walk your spiritual journey with more understanding and realization of how powerful you are.

The three ways your cat is trying to push you further along in your awakening are:

1. Showing heightened or intensified behavior
2. Reflecting your own life topics back at you
3. Manifesting your physical symptoms

We will go into them in more detail in the following section. But first let me say that your cat is not doing any of this to punish you or out of spite. Instead, it is the greatest proof of her unwavering love for you. That is why the Universe put her by your side!

Let's look at these three areas of your cat being your wisdom teacher. This is how your cat nudges you to pay attention – not to her, but to yourself and your own life.

1. YOUR CAT SHOWS HEIGHTENED BEHAVIOR:

When cats want to get your attention and tell you something, it is not always easy for them. They cannot „talk" to you and explain their concerns or wishes. So they will get your attention any way they can - and very often that is by increasing the frequency, tonality, or urgency of a certain behavior.

This can be anything from increased meowing, sometimes even in the middle of the night, keeping you awake without you under-standing why your kitty is so vocal. Or your cat shows some kind of anxiety, or restlessness, running around, scratching or vying for your attention more than usual. Or your cat will eat and eat, and keep begging for food, for no apparent reason.

Any cat behavior that is out of the usual, can fall into this category. It can be anything from excessive rubbing against people or objects, increased or obsessive grooming, intensified toilet behavior, scratching or biting, excessive playing, or even starting fights with a fellow cat. Anything that is heightened or intensified should be a warning sign that the cat is either not happy or stressed out with her life or her environment – or that YOU are not happy or fulfilled in your life! In the context of your spiritual awakening, intensified cat behavior is usually a big sign that your cat wants to get your attention to tell you something about yourself that you are not noticing.

A little disclaimer: As I explained in the beginning of this book, our cats are subject to the same cosmic energies that affect us, thereby causing cat ascension symptoms, such as irritability, restlessness, or emotional ups and downs. This should always be taken into account. If you notice ascension symptoms in yourself, then the likelihood is that your cat has some as well. But apart from – or in addition to – that, your cat usually wants to tell you something with her behavior and alert you to the fact that you are not in balance.

A very common theme reported by my clients during the heavy 2020 lockdowns was their cat „wanting more attention". In times of home office, their cats would interrupt them during their work time. They thought their cat wanted to be petted or get more attention, but in reality, that was far from it. Instead, the cats picked up their humans' stress and worries during the lockdown, as well as the distress and fear from the collective of humanity. As a result, they tried to be there for their people, to help them through these difficult times. So by „demanding attention" when their person was at the computer, the cats actually wanted to point out that their person was not happy.

They would walk in front of the computer screen when their person was not comfortable in a zoom video call. They would step over the keyboard when their person was stressed out with their project, and they would knock over their computer mouse when their person was in dire need for a break.

So whenever you think that your cat is „bothering" you while you do something, and that your cat wants attention – think again! Do you have a cat walking all over you when you are working? Then chances are that you are not happy with what you are doing. And the more exasperated you get with your cat when she bothers you, the more the cat heightens her behavior! So next time that happens, change your perspective of it. It does not mean that your cat feels neglected or wants your attention for herself. On the contrary, your feline picks up your stress or internal pressure while you are working on your project, when you get tired, or even bothered by your work. Your cat notices your mood swings or your inner dilemma, and wants to tell you that it is time for a break!

Of course this doesn't just pertain to your current work project, but for everything you do. Your cat will notice and feel that you are not happy with your job, your profession, or whatever it is that you do for a living.

While cats understand that we humans have to „do things" in order to make a living, they also intrinsically know that we are not in this world to suffer and just get by. Their soul knows that we are here for something bigger, and that we have a calling inside of us. So your cat will instinctively KNOW when you are not aligned with your work and when you should be doing something else that would make you happier – like following your calling.

2. YOUR CAT REFLECTS YOUR OWN LIFE TOPICS:

The second way of getting your attention – and helping you out with your emotional „stuff" – is for your cat to reflect your own life topics back at you. This is important, because we humans hold a lot of unresolved emotions in our energy body and even physical body. They keep our energy from flowing, and our unconscious mind blocks us from moving ahead in life. These stored emotions are anything from old engrained programs from childhood, societal imprints, or limiting beliefs that hold us back from going into the New and living our best life. We also come with old karmic burdens and emotional issues that we have buried deep down and dragged along for years... either from this life and our childhood, or from our past lives.

The beautiful thing is that your cat knows you have unresolved „stuff" you carry around. She can feel it weighing you down and keeping you from moving ahead. So your cat will do whatever she can to point out your limiting and burdensome life topics.

If your cat shows alarming and completely new behaviors, such as being depressed, retreating a lot, being sad, not eating well, not feeling much happiness, etc., then typically your cat is reflecting that YOU are currently not experiencing much joy in your life. You are too sad, too retracted, too unmotivated. So a seemingly depressed or introverted cat will most likely reflect a human who is experiencing these same symptoms or emotions in their life.

Or it can be just the opposite: an aggressive cat is usually a reflection of a person who is impulsive, irritable, angry and ready to „bite off someone's head" when approached at the wrong moment. When people come to me with cats that are „dominant" and fighting with others, I quickly find out that there is this same pattern in the family: a person who is taking out their frustration on the other people in the family, who is irritable or harbors anger deep inside.

By the same token, when two cats are not getting along, or suddenly not getting along anymore, they almost always show me that their humans are not getting along! That the spouses are „hissing" at each other and „growling" a lot. That their humans have lost some of their loving feeling for each other and treat each other with negativity or lack of respect. When cats are fighting each other, they usually have a very simple message for their humans: „We are your mirror; by fighting, we are just showing you how you treat each other! When you find your mutual respect and love for each other again, then we will get along as well".

There are countless more examples of cats reflecting their humans. For instance, a cat that is being mobbed by other cats, and subsequently goes into hiding or retreats a lot, will most likely reflect a person who lets other people walk all over them. This is a person who doesn't stand up for themselves or has low self-esteem. Someone who doesn't show themselves fully to the world and lets others run the show. Someone who hides from the world and doesn't dare to shine their light and stand in their power.

And then, of course, there are countless cases with a „litter box problem". One of the biggest issues that people come to me for help is that their cat does her business outside of the litter box. And while that of course does NOT correlate to a person who doesn't use the toilet, it still is a very clear message of a cat to her person. But mostly, the human doesn't get the meaning of what is behind that weird cat behavior. When your cat puts her business outside the cat toilet, then it is a very drastic way of telling you that something is wrong. The cat probably tried to show you in many other ways, but it was so subtle that you didn't get the memo. And thus the cat has to step it up and stops using the litter box – which is a sure way to get your attention!

So what is behind it? Well, the answer usually lies in the „where" the peeing takes place. I worked with cats who peed in front of their person's closet or the bathroom mirror, meaning in those places where their humans (mostly women) are getting dressed or made up in the morning, with an anxiety of „having to look good". By peeing on that spot, your cat wants to tell you how you are too stressed out or excessively worried about your looks.

When the cat pees under your work desk, then this is a sure sign that you are not happy with your work! When the cat pees on your couch or in your bed, then this is a good indication that something is troubling you or you are stressed out at night. In any case, it usually has to do with how YOU feel in these places where the cat marks the spot.

I want to add a little disclaimer here: a cat that pees outside the litter box might also have a physical problem (such as bladder infection or urinary tract blockages), and it should *always* be checked by your vet. But when your vet gives your cat a clean bill of bladder health, then please go inwards and find out what the places she pees on have to do with you and your inner tensions.

There are, of course, many other unresolved life topics your cat might show you such as compulsive behavior, or restless sleeping, or emotional overeating, or being distrustful of others, or not being settled in life. The list goes on and on, and I think you get the picture. Your cat can mirror you in many countless ways, and by doing so, she always wants to point out the issue to you, so that you can seek resolution for it.

Why your cat is a reflection of you

There are two different reasons why your cat may be showing you your own life topics.

One, either your cat notices an unresolved theme in you, through observing your behavior, and then consciously starts to play it back to you. She wants to hold a mirror in front of your face, in the hope that you will recognize yourself in your HER behavior. Many times, we humans are so wrapped up in the things we „need" to do, that we don't notice what is bubbling deep down inside of us, or which unresolved emotions or stories makes us suffer internally. These can come to the surface in many ways: for instance in compulsive overeating, or excessive house cleaning, or inner restlessness, or chewing your fingernails. Your cat knows there is a deeper issue and starts copying your behavior, so that you can recognize yourself in her, and then do something about it!

Two, there are cats who do not consciously mirror you, but who just „coincidentally" have some of the same issues you have. In this case, the Universe actually sent you a cat that came with the same life topics and unaddressed issues as you so you can work through them together. For instance, not being settled in life, mistrust, being anxious, or not fitting in – the list is endless! In this case, you will attract a cat into your life who has the same themes so that you recognize yourself in the cat, and then can start addressing them – for the benefit of both of you!

How does that all serve you, you may say? Well, it is really easy: just see the theme you both share as a wonderful learning experience that you can now master together with your cat. It is all about acknowledging these topics, addressing them, healing them, and then leaving them behind you. As you are letting go off your old „stuff" and its underlying emotions, so will your cat. And it can be a beautiful joint journey of trusting and healing.

While cats understand that we humans have to „do things" in order to make a living, they also intrinsically know that we are not in this world to suffer and just get by. Their soul knows that we are here for something bigger, and that we have a calling inside of us. So your cat will instinctively KNOW when you are not aligned with your work and when you should be doing something else that would make you happier – like following your calling.

3. YOUR CAT MANIFESTS YOUR PHYSICAL SYMPTOMS:

So far, we have talked about how your cat tries to get your attention through intensified behavior, and how she may reflect your own life topics back at you – so that you recognize that certain areas in your life need reconciling and healing.

However, there is a third way of getting your attention, and this is the escalation of the prior stages: your cat may actually manifest an illness or a physical condition.

It is a well-known fact that sometimes our pets take on our own physical problems and manifest them in an attempt to alleviate us and take them off our shoulders, as a shared burden so-to-speak. There are cases where a person has cancer, and their cat or dog will develop cancer as well. This is the highest form of love and service our pets have for us, and it is certainly also the most drastic expression of it. But let us go into the „lighter" cases and those areas where our pets want to show us the areas of our body where we need emotional healing.

Before we go deeper into the physical body, it is important to know that there is a correlation between the physical and the metaphysical. While our body appears solid, it really consists of energy and vibration at its very core. So it is easy to understand that any irritation or distortion you have in your energy field – be it emotional or mental – will have an impact on your body. In my daily healing work, I understand that behind mostly every physical problem, lies an emotion. When you find the emotion or the emotional topic behind the physical problem, and resolve it, then your body can go into its natural and in-built regeneration mode.

The interesting thing is that each body part and each organ stands for a certain emotion or topic. So your cat may develop a problem in a certain body part, either because you have that same problem, or in order to help you with that specific life topic.

For instance, your cat might develop stomach problems if that is an area of yours that gives you trouble. Or she may take on your bladder infection or the topics that are usually showing through the bladder. This organ stands for keeping things in, not letting go, being overly controlled, or being „filled" with an emotion that you have no outlet for. Just as these topics will cause bladder irritation in humans, it also does so in cats. So if your cat has problems with urination or a bladder infection, then look into yourself: is there anything you are „holding in" or that makes you feel „bottled up"? Are you overly controlled with your emotions or are there things that you are not „letting out"?

Now that you are familiar with the concept that a lot of illnesses, problems, or weaknesses in your body are usually an outward manifestation of an internal struggle or emotional issue, let me give you more examples of what cats usually manifest for their people. It would be too much to go into the entire list of emotions and correlating body parts, but I will list a few that show up quite frequently in my work.

Skin problems have to do with „not feeling well in your own skin" or not being settled in who you are. I had clients with skin rashes, who told me that their cats were licking themselves bald in certain spots, or also developed a skin rash, hair loss, etc. When I asked the cats if they could let go off the emotion behind it, the cats responded that they wanted their person to let go of their emotional skin rash as well. When the person was not ready to face their issue behind their rash, then the cats would typically also keep licking their bald spot.

Throat problems are also a widespread issue among my clients. When you have a sore throat or a closed throat chakra, this usually stands for not speaking your truth, or „swallowing" what you really want to say, or not being able to communicate well – be it with other people or the Universe. Your cat will pick up this closed throat chakra and either develop a throat problem as well, or she might even start to pee outside the litter box. A lot of times such a

„peeing elsewhere" just means that the cat cannot express herself to you any other way than resorting to the drastic peeing measure, because she feels she is not „getting seen or heard" otherwise – which may be a reflection of yourself not feeling seen or heard by others.

Here are a few more emotional meanings behind issues with certain body parts. These have the same meaning for people as they do for cats. Problems with legs, knees, or feet stand for not being well settled in life, or not finding your path. Eye problems signify „not seeing your path clearly", or „not wanting to see all the bad things around you". Ear problems stand for „not hearing your guidance", or „not wanting to hear something that people say". The pancreas stands for „keeping yourself from the good life", and the liver for „not being able to process things well". Stomach issues obviously stand for „not being able to stomach something". The lungs and bronchi stand for pent-up suffering, or „not allowing yourself to breathe". The kidneys stand for „letting things get to you", the spleen for „pent-up anger", the colon for „not being able to process things", etc. This list goes on and on, but I think you get the picture.

Why does your cat show you these issues?

Let's take a step back from all these details and look at the bigger picture. What is the main reason for your felines either pushing you with their behavior or manifesting physical illnesses? Well, they usually feel you are suppressing or not noticing these issues in your life, so they step up and act. Their point is to get you to „wake up and smell the coffee"... or, in this case, to wake up and deal with your „stuff". It is really very simple:

When your cat „acts up" – she is showing you the way!

Remember to not be upset if your cat points these things out to you. By doing so, she acts as your coach and wisdom guide, so that you see what is going on in your life, maybe behind the scenes in your subconscious and largely unnoticed by you.

Cat quote:

„*I love you so much. I am sorry I am causing trouble sometimes. Please forgive me when I do something `wrong', but it is my job to push you. Please don't forget to appreciate yourself and how much you have grown. You are wonderful the way you are. Just do your thing and don't wonder about what other people say. Do what brings you joy and pursue the reason you are here on Earth. With so much love for you – **Simba**.*"

My personal journey: Following my purpose

In 2018, I finally quit my job and dove into the experience of being a full-time cat whisperer, healer, and coach. I realized soon what my niche or specialty was: to find the common thread between a cat and their human, and how cats are nudging and guiding us on our life path.

I developed my signature `Holistic Cat Therapy', which was a unique mix of animal communication (asking the cat what they she needed or wanted to say), energy healing (helping the cat heal the underlying emotional or physical symptoms), and coaching (working with the cat parent with whatever changes they need to make in their life or the life of their cat). In the beginning, I worked one on one, with each client and cat at a time. Eventually, I saw the underlying pattern, that each and every cat pointed out the same things to their humans: „Please be happy. Please do what you love. Please shine your light. Please wake up to who you truly are. I am here to lovingly push you and to show you the way!"

So I started to put these messages together into classes, group coaching, and finally I knew that I had write books about it, to get the message out to a much wider audience. And here we are!

Of course I wasn't just teaching people to listen to their cats but was also doing so myself. My own cats kept pushing me throughout this entire process of becoming a cat whisperer and coach, and mirrored me whenever needed so I would stay on my highest path and unfold all of my potential.

At the time I lived with three beautiful and precious cats – Lennie, Lisa, and Jamie. As I mentioned before, each one of them had a special task with me, which I understand so much better now! They all helped me in my daily work and with my emotional „stuff". And they worked beautifully together, like clockwork, to show me the areas in my life that still needed attention.

My loving companions of almost 18 years recently all passed away, and I am still reeling from the shock of losing all three of them. But I also know they work for me from the other side of the veil, still guiding me lovingly on my path. These were their individual roles with me:

Lennie was my soulmate. He supported me with everything I did. He carried me emotionally, he was my shadow and my best friend. When I worked, he always sat close to me, giving me an energetic support bubble. His motto was „you don't have to walk your path alone, I am always with you". Lennie was also the one who would literally walk all over my computer keyboard to remind me when it was time to take a break. Or he would step in when he noticed me becoming irritated or stressed, by rubbing himself against me and meowing until I pulled away from whatever stressed me, released my tension, relaxed a bit, and came back into the now. He was my personal coach and therapist, and I always listened to his advice. Not only did I love Lennie deeply, I feel there is a big part of me missing, now that he has passed away.

Lisa was both my female inspiration and my mirror. Her passing opened my eyes even more on how important her task with me was. The way she carried herself, with a natural grace and ease, and her very female antics were a stark reminder to stay in my own female vibes. This was true especially in the times when I worked hard at my executive day job, trying to prove that I was as good and as tough as the guys in the higher management, which I was striving to be part of. In all my outer toughness and male ambitions, I forgot to nurture my soft and feminine side. So Lisa served as a shining example of how you can be both very gentle and feminine, but also stand up for yourself. She taught me that you must show yourself as you are, in all your glory, without trying to pretend to be someone different.

Jamie was always the one pushing me the hardest. He was a rebel who wouldn't comply with any „cannots" but kept pushing the boundaries. He would bite me when I felt irritated, to mirror my own irritated mood. He would fight with his fellow cats to show me I had a squabble with my husband. He would push me any way he could so I would stay on track and in my highest vibration. He made a push for freedom when we moved into a new home that was too small for all of us and made me feel stifled in my creativity. So Jamie broke out of the cat-safe yard and started to freely roam the streets – which inspired me to also free myself from safety nets (in my case „what will people think of me") and to step out of my spiritual closet, by going front and center with my message about cats as divine beings and ascension helpers.

Lennie, Lisa, and Jamie were my loving and supportive companions throughout the first part of my spiritual awakening, and each of them had an essential role in inching me forward. After they passed away, they handed over the baton to little Leon and Sheila, who are my new cat companions for the current part of my spiritual journey. And the Universe sent me exactly these two cats with an ultra high vibration and an enormous zest for life so they can guide me to stay more permanently in the 5th dimensional frequencies.

Leon

CHAPTER 4:
YOUR CAT IS YOUR TRAVEL GUIDE

L et's look at the practical side of things. We have talked about all the things your cat points out to you, but now you are probably asking what it is that actually needs to be done about it. Once again, your cat has a very clear understanding of how to go about this, and I am happy to share it with you in this chapter.

Your cat is your loyal friend and companion

The main reason for your cat to alert you to your old baggage and emotional „stuff" is to get you to step up your awakening process and eliminate your old programming. It is not always easy, because we humans come with tons of unresolved things – not only from this lifetime, but many more lifetimes before that! We come with karmic ties, soul contracts, old vows, energetic bonds, and many limiting beliefs. Consequently, there is so much stuff that needs to be resolved in order for us to move forward. We are actually born at this specific point in time with an accumulative amount of things we need to resolve from all our prior lifetimes – and also themes to undergo for the human collective and all its former lives. You can see this lifetime here as the pinnacle of everything that you have dragged with you over the centuries and couldn't resolve back then. This is mainly because Earth was in the lower frequencies for thousands of years, and the density of the 3rd dimension just wouldn't allow us to resolve our old karmic and energetic ties.

Now that we are moving through the 4th into the 5th dimension, the veils are finally getting thinner. We are able to process things faster, release things more effectively and even easily look into our past lives, so we can recognize and let go of all the old stuff that comes from it.

My guides always tell me: „Everything must go". Just like a winter sale or a going-out-of-business sale, all your old things need to move out of your system and field – both your own energy field and the collective field of humanity. We are all called upon to step up and clear our past in order to move into the future. The New Earth will be free of old karma and will be full of love, joy, purpose, and enlightenment. It goes without saying that we all have to do the inner work if we want to permanently anchor ourselves in the 5D frequencies. And our cats want to actively push and remind us that we still have old clutter to get rid of in order to move into the 5D paradigm.

See your awakening as a joint journey – with your cat being your guide

I have worked with countless women whose cats showed weird behavior, alerting them to the fact that they were not aligned with their purpose or soul path. By working with both the women and the cats, I constitute a wonderful bridge that enables both to go into a lighter, happier version of themselves.

The main thing to remember is that you don't have to go on your journey alone. Your cat is always by your side. And she will be more than happy to step up her part in it and be your trustworthy guide. So don't be shy to ask your cat for help. We are not overburdening our cat companions when we ask them to help us. On the contrary, cats are usually happy when they are seen in their full potential and in all their greatness. So they are more than happy to help.

By now you understand that they are so much more than just fluffy little companions. Cats have a beautiful soul and an important task with us. They were sent to us by divine decree, and they volunteered to be with us during this time of the Great Awakening. Their part is as essential as ours in order to co-create the New Earth for humans, animals, plants, and all the other living, breathing, and conscious beings on this planet.

Enlist your cat for help and guidance

In this last chapter, I am giving you an overview of what your cat wants you to do with all this information. Remember that everything I tell you comes from my hands-on and practical experience with my clients and their cats. I have literally conducted thousands of sessions with beautiful feline souls, and this „guidance system" is the essence of what the cats want me to pass on to their humans. It has proven very efficient for my clients to have measurable results: in short, it leads to happy cats, happy humans, and a smoother spiritual awakening.

Here are 7 steps your cat wants you to take in order for you to reach your full potential and stay aligned with your soul path.

What your cat wants you to do

I have put together your cat's 7-step guidance system, which will help you use your feline companion as your navigation system. I will make it easy for you to follow the steps and do a little self-analysis along the way.

If you want to delve deeper at any point during these 7 steps, you will find reference to further materials, guided meditations and classes - such as tapping into your cat or learning animal communication – at the end of this chapter and also at the end of this book.

For now, I suggest you go through these 7 steps one by one and identify where you stand, what your cat is likely to tell you with her behavior, and how to use this information in order to get on track with your awakening and ascension.

For best results, take out a pen and paper to write down your thoughts and whatever else comes up. I would also advise that you do this in several steps. Either put aside 3 consecutive days to go through it, or do it in one sitting or one weekend. It is up to you how much or how little time you want to dedicate to this – but I assure you that your cat will be very happy and proud of you, the more detailed you work through these steps. So without further ado, here we go.

Your cat's 7 step guidance system:

1. Take your cat's messages seriously
2. Recognize how your cat reflects your issues
3. Go inwards... are you on track?
4. Make changes in the right direction
5. Do what you love
6. Just be happy
7. See your cat as your guide & barometer

This simple but powerful system is what cats always tell me to pass on to their humans. It may sound almost too simple to you, but remember that cats are very much in tune with universal wisdom. For instance, when cats say „just be happy", they intrinsically know that you need to elevate your frequency to the vibration of love and joy – rather than being in the lower vibrations of worry or fear. Or when cats tell their humans to „do what you love", they instinctively know that their human has an important task on this planet, and that it is time to follow their calling and passion.

So without further ado, let's get into the 7 steps, and the adjacent exercises for you.

1. Take your cat's messages seriously:

She really knows what she is talking about! Remember how she is so much more connected to nature's innate wisdom, divine guidance and knowledge of her purpose than you probably are at this stage in your life. Your cat has an instinctive knowing of what we are all supposed to do here.

Don't discard your cat's messages just because it might sound „off" or because she is such a small animal. Not only does your cat have an intrinsic understanding of the Universal flow – but she also knows YOU better than anyone else! She spends more time with you than anyone, she sees right through all your fronts or artificial layers, and she is in close contact with your soul.

Even if your cat may be a playful little kitten, or might seem lethargic, or standoffish, or seems to be more interested in food than etheric stuff. Don't be fooled by the small and outward appearance of your cat. She is a grand being with a mission, and at this special time in human history, your cat means business!

So in one way or another, your cat is most likely trying to get your attention. When understood right, she will point out all the areas in your life where you are not fulfilled and all the topics that are not serving you anymore.

For now, don't worry about understanding your cat correctly. This first step merely constitutes a reminder that your cat has a purpose and a mission with you, and she wants you to take it seriously.

Exercise:

Look or feel into how you see your cat:

- *Do you talk to her in baby talk?*
- *Do you treat her like a little animal that doesn't understand much?*
- *Or do you see her as a grand being, and treat her as your partner?*

Whatever comes out of this exercise, please don't feel bad if you realize that you have treated your cat as a child or as a little furry animal that doesn't understand much. Or if you do baby talk with her. Now you know that your cat is much bigger than you have previously known, and it is easy to change how you interact with her!

Just start talking to her in your normal voice, like you do with a person. Your feline will feel your new resolve and appreciate it. You can now happily accept the fact that your cat wants to be your true life partner and can teach you a thing or two when it comes to your spiritual growth.

After completing this simple starting exercise, you can move on to the next chapter, where you will delve deeper.

2. Recognize how your cat may be reflecting your topics:

This is a big one – and it should always be at the forefront of every-thing. Many of my clients react with guilt or distress when they hear that their cat is taking on their emotional „stuff". They want their cat to just be happy and go about her innocent „cat stuff", rather than reflecting their person's burdens and problems. And you may be tempted to get distraught as well that your cat takes on your is-sues. But remember that your cat is doing that because she loves you and wants to help you. And the best thing you can do is recog-nize and acknowledge the connection she shows you, and then do something about it in your own life. Because once you change that thing in your life – whatever it is - then your cat can let go of the issue as well.

I know that at this point you may say that you want your cat to just let go off all that stuff and just be happy. But trust me when I say that your cat doesn't just want to lie around and eat and play and do nothing. She is far too intelligent for it, and far too advanced in her spirituality and her knowing of the great awakening. Your cat takes her mission seriously and wants to contribute. Remember she is with you for a reason and it is her job to mirror you and your life. Trust and know that your cat is doing what she is doing out of a deep love for you and always for your best interest.

So how do you find that connection between you and your cat? I want to encourage you to sit down with your pen and paper, take some quiet time out, and start jotting down your thoughts. If you have several cats, then do this exercise with each one of them, because they may show you different things about yourself.

Exercise:

Look or feel into the behaviors of your cat:

- *What does she do (out of the ordinary) that worries you?*
- *Has she stepped up or intensified any behaviors lately?*
- *How does your cat mirror you with her behaviors, quirks, and antics?*
- *Where do you recognize yourself in her?*
- *Does she manifest any physical symptoms in body areas where you have a weakness as well?*

Once you have written down your thoughts, go through your notes and let it sink in a bit. Have you identified any behaviors or topics your cat reflects back at you? Does it dawn on you why she is showing a certain behavior lately?

If yes, then great! Find comfort in the fact that now you have something to work with and can tackle whatever came up. So when you are ready and done with this part, then you can go to the next step.

3. Go inwards... are you on track?

This is an essential step in your journey. Most of the time we are so busy with what we are doing in our daily lives, that we don't take the time to go inwards, to reflect and sense if we are on track. We forget to connect to our true selves, our purpose and our soul path, so that we can grow and become the highest expression of ourselves.

Even if you are already advanced on your spiritual path and know what you want, I still encourage you to go through this exercise again, because you might find new angles, new thoughts and, in any case, some inspiration.

Exercise:

What your cat wishes for you is that you take some time out, go inwards, and feel into yourself:

- *Are your truly happy with what you are doing?*
- *Are you happy with who you are?*
- *Are you living life on your terms – or a life that your peers, family, or society expects from you?*
- *Are you contributing to the betterment of this world?*
- *Do you feel content – or do you have a yearning to do something different?*
- *Do you feel aligned with who you want to be?*

Again, after finishing your notes, sit back and take a look at them... and let it sink in. Don't overthink it, but rather feel it with your heart. What feels right about it? What does not sit right with you?

What, on your list, do you want to let go of? And what is the direction you want to go? When you are done with this exercise, then you can move on to the next step.

4. Make changes in the right direction:

Take control of the areas in your life that you just identified in the last exercise. Think about what you can do about it. What can you adjust immediately, and what do you wish to change in the long run? There is always a NOW point where you can make a powerful decision to change something in your life. You don't have to wait for tomorrow, or next week, or an opportune time in your life. The moment of change is always NOW. Everything happens in the now, everything starts in the now.

So if you can, make a powerful intention or choice to do something about those areas or topics in your life that don't serve you anymore!

If there are more than one, then start with the easiest one to tackle. Or start with the one core issue that everything else revolves around: for many women, this is the topic of self-love or the limiting belief that „I am not good enough". This engrained belief is usually the root of everything else. It will result in you not showing yourself to the world in all your glory, in dimming your light, in not developing your gifts, in not trusting your abilities, in not stepping out into the world, and so on.

You may say this is a big task to work on – your self-worth or self-love - and yes, it is. But you have to start somewhere, and as always, the best moment is right now. So just take your first steps in changing that very behavior that your cat showed you is „off" or needs amending. When your cat sees your goodwill and senses your inner resolve, then she will breathe a sigh of relief and scale down her „off" behavior as well.

Our cats do understand that we humans are complex creatures, and that we cannot change overnight. So they don't expect you to go into full-fledged „I am going to change everything" mode. They also understand perfectly that we humans cannot let go of our old wounds, our habits of self-sabotage, or our emotional stuff right away or without doing some serious inner work.

But the cats do want us to get started! So the moment you prove to your cat that you are willing to do something about the topic she shows you, your cat will be satisfied... for now. All they want to see is that you are taking a step in the right direction. And they are smart enough to feel your change of energy, your willingness to heal, or the new behavior that you are going to establish in the place of your old program.

How should you tackle your issues? Well, it all starts with resolve and a powerful intention to do something about it. After that, there are numerous ways of going about it, and we won't be able to go through all of them in the framework of this book. But I will explain in the last chapter how you can find help and more guidance in letting go of your old „stuff".

For now, it is important for your cat to feel your determination and intention to do something about your own life topics, and she will feel the change in you. Most cats will then also step down their behavior a little bit, just to also show you some good will and that they understand your good intentions.

That being said, some cats may be impatient and still continue to show you their „odd" behavior, even if you are taking your own steps in the right direction. In that case, I would advise you to sit down with your cat and tell her that you are going to need some time, and that she should be patient with you.

And on that note, I want to assure you that your cat understands everything you say! Maybe not every single word or not very complex and theoretical constructs, but cats do understand our words, our emotions, and the intentions behind what we say. So you can talk to your cat the same way you talk to a human being. If you tell her you need some more time to resolve your issues, she will understand. Most cats are glad to just see you get off to a good start!

Exercise:

This one is all about you and your desired changes:

- *Write down 3 minor things (or behaviors) that you can start changing today.*
- *Write down the biggest goal what you want to change in your life in the next 6 months.*
- *Then tell your cat you understood her messages and that you are willing to make changes. She will be happy and proud of you!*

By completing this exercise, you are making a big leap into the New You and aligning yourself with your higher path. Now you can go into the „how" you will be changing your life, which we will address in the next step.

5. Do what you love:

This is one of the main things cats tell me: that their humans are not happy with what they do, and not fulfilled with their jobs or their way of life. Your cat knows that there is so much better for you out there in the world, and all your cat wants is for you to *do what you love and love what you do.*

It sounds simple enough, and for cats it seems fairly simple when they give us that message. They watch us slave away at our computer, or do chores that we really cannot stand. They wonder why we humans are so busy with things that really don't make us very happy. So for them the message is clear: dear human, please do what you love!

What they mean by that is not just doing happy things around your house. They really mean business and talk about „the bigger picture" we have discussed earlier in the book:

Your cat wants you to be embrace your gifts and powers, to develop your superpowers, to find your calling – and then for you to go follow your purpose!

Remember the exercise in step 3 where you were going inwards and jotting down how you feel about who you are and what you do, and how you want to show up in the world? Well, this is where we will get to the subject of your life purpose. Your cat intrinsically knows that there is something you are doing here on Earth, your unique fingerprint and your „piece of the puzzle", so-to-speak. We touched upon this in the very first chapter.

Your feline companion is deeply aware of her own mission – which she truly lives, breathes and feels. And she knows that you have one, too. For your cat, it is crystal clear that she can do her job and be happy doing it. And guess what? She wishes the same for you!

So where do you stand on your life purpose? Are you aware what it is or what your contribution is? If yes, then great – all you have to do is going about it in whatever way is possible for you in your current life situation. Not everyone can just leave their job and delve into their passion or build their own business overnight. Nor would I recommend doing it! But you can start with small steps and slowly build up your business, your new career, your side job, or whatever it is that you want to do.

For many people, it is not even about switching careers or making drastic life changes. Their purpose may revolve around helping out others in their community or bringing more joy to people. In this case, there is nothing to be changed in their life – except for them being more of who they are.

If you are not aware of your life purpose, then now is a perfect time for you to tune into it and find it. This is typically not something that you do overnight. However, I will give you one example of how to find out what your purpose or calling is, in the following exercise.

Exercise:

Sit down with a bit of time and journal about what you LOVE doing. It's important that you write from the heart and not from the head. Take this exercise easy. Don't overthink your answers. Instead, put the pen on the paper and just let it flow out.

- *Which activities come easy and natural to you?*

- *What makes your heart sing?*

- *What can you do better than anyone else?*

- *What makes you truly happy?*

- *What do you plan on doing after retirement?*

- *What would you love to contribute to the world?*

- *How do you touch people, or animals, or plants, or the environment by how you think, what you do and how you show up in the world?*

This exercise was a big one! Know that whether you have a long list or a short one, size doesn't matter. You may want to put down your journaling for awhile, go drink some coffee or go for a walk – and then after your break, pick your notes up and read through them.

Is there a common thread between your answers? Is there anything that pops up more often than other things? Which of your answers makes your heart warm and puts a smile on your face?

Your purpose might hit you upside the head, or shyly peek through what you wrote. But whatever feels GOOD to you and excites you likely has to do with your main purpose.

You don't need to rush this step, and you can always came back to this later. The main point I want you to take away from this is to become aware of and aligned with your purpose. And you can be assured that your cat will notice it when you start doing what you love, because it will make you a brighter, happier, and more fulfilled you. Which, in turn, means that you will have a happier and more balanced cat by your side!

So whether you have now fully found your purpose, or just starting to get an idea about it, you can always move on the next point. This one is closely related and helps you become more aligned with your true self and who you want to be in this world.

6. Just be happy:

This sounds like a simple advice that is easy for your cat to say, but it is not something you can just DO... or is it?

As a matter of fact, this is the number one wish that cats have for their humans: to be happy. It sounds very simple but there is so much truth in this statement. And it really ties in neatly with the prior wish your cats have for you: do what you love... and then you will be happy with what you do and who you are.

Most of my clients who come to me with cat problems, tell me that they just want their cat to be happy and would go to great lengths to help them. But they are thinking in terms of more toys or more playtime, or letting their cat go outdoors, or bringing in another cat companion. They want to DO something for their cat to be happy – thinking it is something tangible that they can change. But they are in for a good surprise when I tell them the following: „*Your cat will be happy, when you are happy*".

Most people get stumped when they first hear it because it goes against everything they have done so far. But really, it makes so much sense, doesn't it? You and your cat are a team. You are closely entwined with each other, and your cat loves you more than anything else. So why would your cat not want you to be happy? And how could your cat ever be happy, if you are constantly stressed out or discontent with yourself or hate your job?

So it is actually not surprising that the number one wish of each and every cat I have spoken to is the simple but powerful advice: „Dear human, I just want you to be happy". And by happy, your cat does not mean silly laughing or you having a fleeting happy moment but rather a deep feeling of being content with who you are and what you do. Happy in your overall life and with the path that you chose.

Remember, your cat can be a good barometer for your own happiness level. If you have a cat that is constantly irritated, stressed out or restless, look into yourself. Where are you stressed out, restless, unfulfilled, and not happy with your life? Your cat knows and notices it so much faster than you when you are not aligned with your purpose and not happy with where you are in life.

Happiness is also not just a state of mind, but also a state of your vibration. Everything is energy, and we are vibrational beings. When you align yourself more permanently with the frequencies of love and joy, then you are one step closer in your spiritual awakening. The ascension process is all about elevating our vibration and anchoring ourselves in the 5th dimensional frequencies. In order to do so, you need to find a higher set point of overall happiness in your life, which in turn elevates your vibration, which in turn aligns you with your purpose, calling, and highest soul path.

I understand that being happy is not something you can do at the flip of a switch. Nor do I want you to suppress your negative emotions or your shadow side. As I have shared with you before, when we go through our spiritual awakening, there is a a lot of emotional baggage that comes up, and that needs to be dealt with. I've been there, and done it, and I know it is not always easy to switch back into the „lighter" moods, after you have done a lot of feeling in, healing and exonerating of your past traumas or past lifetimes. Some spiritual teachings suggest that you need to be joyful and happy all the time... while others tell you to delve deeply into your shadow work. These conflicting statements are confusing for many awakening souls, and there is really no right or wrong to both schools of thought.

My approach is somewhere in the middle: Be happy or in the higher frequencies as much as you can – and deal with your negative emotions or destructive patterns whenever they come up. There is no use in suppressing your true emotions, because all you'll do is push them into your subconscious, where they will sit and cause some kind of reaction later on. This, in turn, results in physical symptoms or emotional outbursts when you least expect them... and adds to your stress level.

I have done so many healing sessions with clients that I know that old „stuff" wants to be seen, heard and then released. But I also know that we can do it faster and more efficiently now in these times of lifting veils and dimensional shifts. Often it is enough to sit with it, acknowledge it – and then let it go. No need for painful re-iteration of past traumas or digging deep into old traumatic lifetimes. I usually let my clients feel into it – recognize it – and then release it.

After the session, you can go back into the higher vibrations, lighter emotions and more elevated thoughts.

As a good rule of thumb: my spirit guides tell me it is enough if we are in a lighter and happier mood around 60% of our time. That sets us onto a path of overall elevation and spiritual growth, as a person and as a soul. And it is absolutely doable in your normal, everyday life to stay or shift into happier thoughts at least 60% of your day.

Exercise:

So how do you go about just being happy? This could fill yet another book, but let me name a few easy exercises you can do on a daily basis to embody a lighter and happier vibe:

- *Think happier thoughts. Whenever you catch yourself having a negative thought that brings you down, say „cancel" and replace it with a happier thought.*

- *Stay away from too much media and things that bring down your vibration. Instead embrace more things throughout your day that make you feel good.*

- *Practice gratitude. Be grateful for all the good things in your life. Start in the morning with giving thanks for warm water and a cup of coffee, and give thanks throughout your day for having a job or a car, for a good meal or a great opportunity. And most of all, be grateful for having your loved ones and your wonderful cats in your life!*

- *Focus on the things you want to see in the world, rather than thinking about all the things you don't want or like.*

Being happy is easier than you think, even if you are stuck in a job you don't like or face bills you think you cannot pay. There is so much goodness around us that we take for granted, and that we are not thankful for. The moment you start praising the good things in your life, you will notice a positive change.

It is important to know that your thoughts come first and your emotions follow. So if you don't know how to just „turn on" the emotion of happiness, then start with a positive thought. The more you think about happy things, the more you will actually FEEL happy! Gratitude is the easiest thing to use when you feel yourself slipping from your elevated mood. There is always something to be grateful for. Think of it, list it, thank it, and your mood will be lifted instantly.

In order for us to elevate in the ascension process and become a happier, lighter version of ourselves, one of the main steps is to raise our vibration on a permanent basis. So every time you feel yourself slip into a lower vibration, or a mood that doesn't feel good, then catch yourself in the process, and change your thoughts into a lighter mode.

And lastly, for you as a cat lover: if all else fails, and you cannot think of anything that makes you happy, then turn to your cat! Talk to her, pet her or think about her. Think about all the joy she brings you, and how she loves you dearly and unconditionally. This should bring a smile on your face, if nothing else did.

7. See it as a joint journey, with your cat as your guide:

By now you have a pretty good understanding of what your cat is reflecting in your life, and which of your life topics you want to work on, transmute, and let go. I actually prefer not to call it „working on yourself" but rather see it as a journey into the New, by letting go of the Old that no longer serves you.

The beautiful thing about your journey is that you don't have to walk it alone! You can enlist your cat for help and guidance. She is already by your side as your loyal friend and companion, and she is more than happy to show you the way.

How does this work? Well, you can be sure that your cat will keep showing you the areas where you are still not fully on track or where you are holding back.

As a rule of thumb, whenever your cat „acts up", she is actually showing you the way! And you can take her as your barometer on your journey. When your cat is relaxed and happy, then most likely you are on track and exactly where you need to be on your journey. On the other hand, when your cat slips back into the behavior that we identified earlier, or when she keeps holding the mirror in front of your face, then she is telling you that you are not on track and need to do more of your inner work.

With her fine antennas for your emotional and mental wellbeing, your cat will always know when you are not happy or relaxed. So she will be your living reminder and your assistant, catching you when you need to pull back and relax. Just pay attention to your cat, like you would to a barometer telling you the temperature of the day.

When your cat keeps coming to you with increased meowing, restlessness, not wanting to settle down... when she keeps rubbing herself against you, interrupting you in your work, then she is telling you to stop doing what you are doing in that moment, and just take a breather. In this case, relax, step back from what you are doing and come back to the moment. It helps to pull yourself out from the situation where you went into too much stress or tension. By breathing and focusing on just „being" for a moment, and cuddling with your cat for a few minutes, you bring yourself back to center. Then you can return to the task you were just doing, but with less tension and a higher energy level.

When it comes to more deep-seated life topics, you can consider yourself lucky to have a „mirror cat" who reflects your unresolved topic back to you. I am saying „lucky" because she will always let you know where you stand in your quest to overcome and transmute that topic. Trust her instincts. All in all, you can see it as a wonderful joint journey to overcome these issues together. As you start growing and letting go of your emotional „stuff", so will your cat. If your journey is about learning to show yourself to the world more, then you can both take your small steps towards showing up with more confidence – you with your co-workers and in your community, and your shy cat with the other cats around her. While you might get more respect and make new connections at your workplace, your cat will not hide under the sofa anymore but sit among the other cats more often. And you can both be happy with each other's progress and learn to enjoy the journey together. Your feline will be immensely proud of you.

Exercise:

This one is not an exercise to sit down and journal about, but rather an ongoing exercise in understanding and interpreting your cat's behavior. So whenever your cat seems restless and you feel she is trying to say something, then ask yourself the following questions:

- *How does your cat push you or reflect you in that moment?*

- *What are your emotions or thoughts in that moment?*
- *Then adjust your thoughts and/or emotions to a happier and lighter version – and thank your cat for bringing it to your attention.*

You can practice this from now on, and you will be surprised at how many times your cat will „catch you" in the act of not being happy, or not being aligned with what you truly want.

Once you recognize your feline companion as your emotional barometer or wisdom teacher, your life will become much easier, and your joint journey can be a magnificent one.

Your cat is your guide

This concludes your cat's simple but powerful 7-step guidance system, to help you in your awakening process and becoming a happier, lighter New You.

If you want to go further on your quest to better understand your feline, to learn animal communication, to heal or transmute your unresolved life topics, and to truly find your life purpose, then come see me and the cats at the Feline Soul Academy.

You can find more inspiration, free meditations, and further resources, as well as classes, group programs, and coaching here:

www.felinesoulacademy.com
www.felinesoulacademy.com/courses/cat-communication
www.felinesoulacademy.com/courses/your-cat-is-your-guide

Cat quote:

*„Dear human, I am always here for you – all of your cats are. We will continue to push you until you learn to trust your inner voice and see your path laid out in front of you. We love you so much, and we push you because you once asked us to do so – in a former life. We want you to walk your path in love and joy. Listen to your intuition and your gut feeling. You can do this! With so much love for you – **Pride**."*

My personal journey: Stepping into my power

So here we are, in the 2020's, navigating the stormy waters of ascension and deep transformation. When the next big wave of awakening hit ALL of humanity in 2020, it turned upside down the world as we knew it. The majority of people are still asleep, not understanding the bigger picture behind the massive changes we are seeing on a global scale. But many awakening souls are coming „online" in masses now. In times of lockdowns and social distancing, people started to go inwards, and realized what was really important: family, purpose, and inner growth, rather than running and chasing something outside of themselves. Many were forced out of their jobs, but realized that the challenge was also a gift in disguise because it enabled them to do what they loved and start over, rather than staying in a job that made them miserable. The big opportunity of the pandemic was that it prompted all of us to look *within* and to start changing from *within*.

Personally, I found myself working more with *people* rather than *cats* as of 2020. During the first lockdowns, many clients reached out to me for help, reporting that their cats were acting up and having emotional problems. But in truth, these cats were awakening and stepping up to their purpose: to push their humans to wake up!

What the cats showed me was amazing: They could feel their humans being unsettled during the pandemic, and they felt the collective of humanity going into shock, fear, and uncertainty. The cats picked up the collective mood of humans, and they went into full-blown purpose and guidance mode. They said it was time for their humans to awaken to their true selves, to connect to their calling and to embrace their gifts. In order to be heard, the cats stepped up their efforts in „pushing" their humans (aka „acting up"). They wanted their human companion to look into their unresolved emotions and topics, so that they would level up, get out of their comfort zone, and make bigger leaps in their spiritual journey.

Since the cats made it clear to me that it was not *them* that needed help, they inadvertently ushered me into working more with their humans. Consequently, my focus shifted to being more of a coach and healer for the cat parents, rather than a healer for their cats. And by doing so, the cats pushed me as well! This new focus forced me to become even clearer in what I relayed to people: the cats did not want me to pass on trivial messages to their humans anymore, but they meant business with their spiritual messages. In my healing sessions with people, I found myself channeling not only their cat's higher selves, but also their dead grandparents or their star families, and telling my clients that they were starseeds or lightworkers and needed to wake up.

So my clients' cats really uplifted me to fully come out of my spiritual closet, and to not only show myself as a spiritual cat whisperer, but also as a healer, channel, medium, and interdimensional starseed. There were moments where my clients were not ready for the channeled messages from „above" coming through me, but their cats would be relentless. They made it very clear that their person needed to hear it! With the cats forcing my hand, I grew to overcome my spiritual shyness and just told my clients the whole truth of what was presented to me. Whereas before, I had toned down messages or their origins, to make it more digestible for my unawakened client. The cats no longer tolerated that.

I started to accept that when a spiritual message comes through me, either from a cat's higher self or from divine channeling, then the person needs to hear it. At the very least, I would plant a seed in my client for it to bloom later. Even if the person was still doubtful, their cat would assure me that I had done the right thing and been an immense help for both of them.

So it was really the cats that I worked with who taught me to step into my own power and speak my truth. And before I knew it, I had become a spiritual teacher and coach, who helped awakening cat lovers to connect with their purpose, their higher guidance, and their cats.

Sheila

CHAPTER 5:
YOUR BEAUTIFUL JOINT JOURNEY

Congratulations, you are now officially „in the knowing" about your cat, which takes you many steps ahead of other people in their awakening. Just by understanding how you can harness the power and the wisdom and the love of your cat, in order to progress in your spiritual awakening, you can move much faster than before.

So where should you go from here? Assuming that a good part of your spiritual journey is still ahead of you, it is up to you to choose how you will walk down your life path. Even if you are aware of your purpose and your calling and what you want to create in your life, you can choose to go fast or slow. Imagine your life path like a highway in front of you. The path has been laid by your soul and by your intentions. But whether you drive it down at full speed in the left lane, or whether you make the trip into an adventure, stopping for regular coffee breaks and sightseeing, is completely up to you. Some people choose to take a zigzag course on their highway, and they frequently stop to smell the flowers by the roadside. There is no limit to how you walk down your life path, so remember that the „how" is always your choice. And also remember that your cat is sitting in the passenger seat next to you, ready to help you navigate or to cheer you on when the road seems too winded or obscured by fog or heavy weather.

Wherever you stand on your journey – at the very beginning or somewhere well in the middle – you are always where you need to be right now! There is no right or wrong, and your higher self is always looking out for you, so that you can never go wrong. This is important to know, so you can build trust in yourself and in the Universe as well as your higher guidance. They are always there for you, even when you feel things are not going as planned or if you seem to have stepped into a pothole on your road. Know that things are always happening FOR you, and not TO you. If you take everything you encounter as a means to learn, grow and change, then life becomes much easier and makes a whole lot more sense.

Your higher guidance – which includes your higher self, the divine realm, and your personal spirit guides – is always there to look out for you. For a moment, imagine and see your higher guidance as the cat parent: just like you as the guardian of your cat know with every fiber of your being that you will always be there for your cat, and she will never have to go without food or shelter or love, this is exactly how your higher guidance is there for you. It's looking out for you, protecting you, and guaranteeing that you will never be without food, shelter, or love. If you can just trust the basic principles that everything will always work out for you, that you are divinely guided and protected every step of your way, then you will emit that frequency into the Universe and uphold or better create that exact scenario.

The guiding principles of this book

Since we are nearing the end of this book, let us look back at the most important points we have covered:

1. The Great Awakening of humanity is in full swing – and our cats are awakening as well.

2. Cats are divine and highly intelligent beings with a beautiful task - to help us awaken to our purpose.

3. Your main purpose at this point is to find your special piece of the puzzle so you can contribute to the whole.

4. Your cat knows you best and understands how you feel, even before you do.

5. Your cat pushes you to tackle your old emotional baggage and things that don't serve you anymore.

6. Your cat is your mirror and wants you to recognize yourself in her behavior.

7. Your cat wants you to be happy and cannot be happy unless you are.

8. Your cat wants you to do what you love and to love what you do.

9. You can always ask your cat for help, so you can both move through this journey together.

10. Your cat is your companion, guide, and wisdom teacher, and serves as your barometer in your awakening.

Now you have the basic principles of traveling your beautiful life journey together with your loving passenger and navigation system – your feline.

When you practice tuning in to your cat on a regular basis, you will get a better feeling of where you stand, and how she is giving you valuable insights into your emotional and mental status.

By applying the above principles, you will not only have a happier cat, but also find yourself being happier as well. Why? Because it means that you are progressing on your journey into your personal „New You" in parallel with the New Earth.

Are you aligned with your purpose and calling?

Throughout the reading of this book, you may have found yourself struggling here and there with your old emotional baggage or with identifying your calling. If you already know your purpose, there may still be a little hesitation or insecurity about how to go about it, or about tweaking it to make it more specific.

If you still don't know your purpose, then it really is time to find and follow it. How? There are several methods and processes you can do in order to find your purpose. One of the easiest ones is to just journal and see what comes out. I want to give you another easy technique of journaling, in order to hone in on your life purpose.

Exercise: Find your purpose

1. *Take a pen and a piece of paper. Write „My purpose" on the top of the blank sheet of paper.*

2. *Set aside some quiet time in your busy day, and breathe for a few minutes, until you become calm and still inside. If you know how to meditate, then do your usual routine and add this exercise at the end of your meditation. If you don't know how to meditate, then I suggest to just sit in silence for a few minutes, with your eyes closed, and then get started.*

3. *Take the pen and write down whatever comes to mind, what your purpose could be. It can be as simple or as complicated as you want. It can be a few words, or an entire sentence. The main thing is to not THINK too much about it, but just let it flow out of your pen. Write as many points on your list as want to come out. You may be exhausted after one page and a half, or you might cover 5 full pages of ideas. Just let it come out naturally, don't force it. Once nothing seems to come to mind — or onto your paper — anymore, then stop writing.*

4. *The last step is the most fun: re-read your list and look for any similarities or words/ concepts that come up the most. This is honing in on your purpose. Whatever you wrote about the most, there is a very good indication that it is what you wanted to know.*

5. *Then write your purpose on a clean sheet of paper, and sit with it. How does it feel? Does it make sense to you? Does your heart say YES? Also feel into your physical body for signs. If it feels constricting in your body, then chances are that your deducted your „purpose" from your mind or headspace. If it feels uplifting, and puts a smile on your face, then you are on the right track!*

For me, this was my very first exercise when I set out to find my purpose. While it felt strange, I followed the procedure and wrote a list of about 3-4 pages. It started simple, and then the points on the list got more and more complicated. At the end, I re-read it and saw that the similarities were working with cats. Most of my ideas revolved around cats. And then I realized that I had summed it up perfectly in the *very first line* that I had written down: „I want to make this a better world for cats".

Of course my purpose has slightly shifted over the years to come. It soon turned into: „Bringing joy to millions of cats". And now, some years later, it shifted to: „Help humans understand how their cat helps them with their awakening". But the base line about cats is the same.

So you see, your purpose can shift and change, and you don't have to set it in stone! What is important is to get started and understand your basic calling, to find your very special piece of the puzzle, and to embrace your personal superpower.

Cat quote:

„I am helping you awaken to your true greatness and your soul mission. Whether you are ready for it or not, the time is now! You are here to help wake other people up! You are an influential person and people listen to you. When you allow yourself to stand in your full power, with all your spiritual gifts, then you inspire others to show themselves as well. My role is to keep pushing you until you fully own your gifts and until you are fully aligned with your soul path. Sending you so much love – **Beltcho.** *"*

My personal journey: The cats are my guides

December 2020 rang in another wave of awakening, with mother Gaia humming like a bell, and strong cosmic energies hitting our planet. Throughout 2021, all of humanity seemed to be pushed to their limits, with global outer turmoil and personal inner purging going on at the same time.

For me, some of my deep-seated emotional „stuff" and old baggage that I thought I had put behind me came back to hit me with full force. I realized that while I had worked through it on a mental and energetic level, there was still some residue in my emotional body as well as an imprint in my physical body.

This was a common theme on a global level. My clients went through the same rocky process, of working through and releasing old emotional patterns and limiting beliefs they thought they had let go a long time ago. The year 2021 kept pushing us to do spring cleaning, where you finally get rid of all the stuff that goes unseen in normal cleaning: dust lying around in dark corners, under rugs, and in drawers long forgotten. Or as my higher guidance kept telling me: everything must go. Like a going-out-of-business sale, where all the shelves need to be cleared out for good, so you can start fresh with a clean slate.

During this process, I also went through physical purging. While I was upleveling fast in my etheric work, spending more time in magical 5D, doing channelings, deep healings, and high-level coachings, my physical body was not up to speed yet. After a high-flying session, it yanked me back into an uncomfortable 3D reality of physical discomfort, aches, and snail speed progress. The gap between the two worlds of 3D and 5D seemed to widen, and I felt like doing the splits more often than not.

It was frustrating and it tested my patience and my belief whether I was doing everything right. However, I understood that I was in the later phase of ascension, where the physical body needs to catch up and adjust to the higher vibrations that you have elevated yourself into. Or where your slow-moving Human Self and your fast-evolving Etheric Self have to come together and merge.

In the middle of these high-flying cosmic energies, solar storms and transformative changes going on in 2021, it was not surprising that I got hit hard with personal losses: my three beloved cat companions of almost 18 years – Lennie, Lisa and Jamie – got sick and all passed away within only 7 months. I was heartbroken, and it all seemed like too much for me to process. But I was also aware of how much it helped me grow and shift my perspective. The crossing of my cats opened me even more to the spiritual realms and the veil between the worlds got even thinner for me. I can still feel and tap into Lennie, Lisa and Jamie, have a conversation with their souls, and even feel their physical presence when I call them in. They are still with me at all times, and only a thin layer away from my physical world. Their gift is that I got to become even more multi-dimensional, and they are now guiding me from the „other side".

Perfectly orchestrated by the Universe, my new kittens, Leon and Sheila, had come into my life at exactly the right time. When Jamie and Lennie passed away, they got to pass the baton to little Leon and Sheila, who took on some of their tasks, while still being their magnificent selves. I could not have possibly planned any of this smooth transition between my older and my younger cats, but it just played out right in front of my eyes. When Lennie crossed over, he told me that everything had to happen this way: that his task was fulfilled, and that I should take the kittens and move on to my new life. The little ones were the perfect companions for the new chapter in my life. Writing this still brings tears to my eyes, but of course I know that Lennie was right.

This gave me great comfort, and I took his passing as the reminder that life is too short to waste it. It gave me the resolve to finally finish my first book and share the cats' important messages with many beautiful awakening souls. So I entered into a new phase of immense clarity on my purpose and a feeling of peace with everything that had happened and where I am going. My energy work is now stronger than ever and my connection with cats is deeper. I trust that I am divinely guided every step of the way and that I am exactly where I need to be right now.

I still ask my cats for guidance every single day: Leon and Sheila in the physical realm, and Lennie, Lisa, and Jamie in the etheric realm. In my daily meditation, I call the five of them in, and thank them for being with me. I ask them how they see me, and if there is anything I need to know. My cats always have valuable advice for me, and they are my biggest cheerleaders, lovingly pointing me the right direction. When I might not see the forest for the trees in a certain issue, they always see clearly and tell me when I am not aligned with something.

I feel lucky and blessed that I have five beautiful and precious cat souls by my side. I love them dearly, and I could not imagine not having them in my life for support. They are currently guiding me go into the stage of soul embodiment, where we bring our Soul Self more fully into our physical vessels, so we can truly shine our light.

At this point in my journey, I am:

- Living and breathing my purpose as a cat whisperer
- Embracing my superpower and speaking my truth
- Helping wonderful cats and cat parents with their awakening
- Fully connected to and evolving with my gifts and talents
- Aware that I am „all in" on this journey and divinely protected
- Following my inner and higher guidance as well as the cats' guidance

As the global awakening of humanity continues, I am very much at ease with who I am and where I stand. And I am truly looking forward to continuing my ascension journey, fully guided by my loved ones and the entire cat collective.

Before you go…

CONCLUSION:
WHERE TO GO FROM HERE

That bring us to the NOW moment where I am wrapping up this book about you, your cat and your awakening. I sincerely hope that you have benefited from it in more ways than one.

I truly wish for you to move smoothly through your ascension process, taking your cat up on her offer to be your guide and navigation system.

My personal story may serve you as an example of all the stages, trials, and tribulations of awakening – but also of all the beautiful successes you can have on your journey. Important to know: it doesn't have to take this long for you! The first wavers of the ascension came online about 30 years ago and they had to do a lot of work on themselves. They were the early „new agers" that paved the way for all of us that followed. The second wavers – like me – woke up in 2012, and it took us „only" 10 years to go through our inner and outer processes.

If you are just getting started with your spiritual awakening, then you are a third waver. And the good news is that you can do it in a very short amount of time! Not only can you learn from the prior waves, but you can benefit from the much higher vibrational frequency that our planet has now, which helps you let go, transmute, and heal your old wounds, patterns, and limiting beliefs much faster than ever before.

You as a cat lover and cat parent have the added bonus of having your very personal feline assistant and ascension coach right by your side, walking with you every step of the way.

So what are your next steps?

If you have worked through the above 7-step cat guidance system, then you are well on your way. You should have a pretty good feeling about where you stand, where you want to go, and who you have by your side as your ascension barometer.

If you continue your journey by yourself, then I am wishing you lots of love, and many great moments of joy and awakening together with your cat companion. For more help or inspiration, you can go to the free resources section in my Feline Soul Academy and look into any information that is helpful for you:

www.felinesoulacademy.com

My Academy is a magical place of transformation and awakening, guided by the cats. You can find everything around cat communication, healing, spiritual awakening & making a true soul connection with your feline.

My invitation to you:

If you wish you understand your cat and her messages better, then I warmly recommend that you learn animal communication. Anyone can learn to speak with their cat and it is much easier than you think. You are welcome to take my course where you learn animal communication in just three days, with all my little secrets on how to talk to cats:

https://www.felinesoulacademy.com/courses/cat-communication

If you need more help in finding or following your purpose, then I recommend you join my ongoing coaching program, where I help you connect to your cat, to your soul self, to your inner and higher guidance, and of course to your purpose and calling. This program also gives you the tools you need to self-heal your past, so you can let go of the Old and go boldly into the New:

www.felinesoulacademy.com/courses/yourcat-yourguide

Whatever you decide to do – go it alone or take up my invitation for learning or coaching – know that I am rooting for you. I can also promise you that your cat will be your loyal and loving companion every step of the way.

We both wish for you to find your piece of the puzzle that you contribute to the Grand Awakening, to fully embrace your superpower, to shine your light, and to walk your soul path with purpose, ease, and joy.

Lots of love,
Sylvie & the Cats

To your beautiful journey

ABOUT SYLVIE STERLING

Cat Expert:

Certified cat psychologist, behavioral counselor, and animal communicator, Sylvie uses a combination of these approaches to help cats with unusual and alarming behavior. Her signature feline soul practitioning brings the cat's body, mind, and soul back into balance.

Intuitive Healer:

After acquiring various certificates in different energy healing methods, Sylvie developed her own healing techniques, which include quantum light healing, emotional healing, and elemental healing. She also taps into powerful 12th dimensional galactic healing frequencies which help clear karma and soul contracts for both cats and people.

Awakening Coach:

In her classes, programs, and retreats for spiritual cat lovers, Sylvie teaches animal communication, feline soul language, and how to navigate spiritual awakening. As a healing coach, she works with cats and cat parents alike, so they recognize how they can best support each other to start living their most purposeful life.

Facebook:

www.facebook.com/yourcatisyourguide

Website:

www.felinesoulacademy.com

www.sylviesterling.com